"An eclectic collection of uplifting poetic musings that help us appreciate who we are and the power of our own potentials."

— *Brandon Royal, award-winning educational writer and author of The Little Blue Reasoning Book*

"I certainly enjoyed reading *Metamorphosis*. These inspiring verses offer enlightening truths of wisdom. They brought me a new understanding of human journey, and a few chuckles, as well."

— *Brian Richards, freelance writer*

"The poetry in the *Purposeful Mind* series really spoke to me and seemed to reflect the learning, the reading, and the knowledge that I have been gaining, and the inner work that I have been experiencing the last several years. It's as if the author has put my life experiences, daydreams, and beliefs into words! Truly amazing! As I read particular poems, the words and phrases gave me further insight into a part of myself, going deeper, with more understanding, and seeing the 'picture' from another point of view. This added to a comfort that I feel about the path I am on, knowing that it is always going 'up'."

— *Sally Parsons, Reiki Master, EFT Practitioner, Artist, facilitator, speaker, teacher*

"I appreciated how expressive these verses are and the wisdom they contain. I have read all five books of this series and can highly recommend them to anyone."

—*Jerry Johnson, Visual Artist*

METAMORPHOSIS

What Else Is Possible?

Purposeful Mind Series – Book Five

Other Books by Helena Kalivoda

AWAKEN!
Your Soul Is Calling

WAKE UP!
Your Heart Is Calling

WAKE UP!
Prosperity Is Calling

Purposeful Mind Series:

CREATION
Accessing Your Untapped Potential

ILLUMINATION
Getting to Know the Invisible You

CONTEMPLATION
Understanding Your Inner World

EVOLUTION
It Is Time for the New You

METAMORPHOSIS
What Else Is Possible?

METAMORPHOSIS

What Else Is Possible?

Purposeful Mind Series – Book Five

HELENA KALIVODA

AUDRENAR BOOKS

METAMORPHOSIS
What Else Is Possible?
Purposeful Mind Series – Book 5

Copyright ©2014 by Helena Kalivoda
Published by Audrenar Books

Library and Archives Canada Cataloguing in Publication

Kalivoda, Helena, -
Metamorphosis / Helena Kalivoda.

Poems.
ISBN 978-0-9877521-4-7

I. Title.

PS8621.A469M47 2012 C811'.6 C2012-902410-4

Editing: Agnes L. Kirby
Cover art: original oil painting by Jaroslav Kalivoda

For more information on this book and other books by Helena Kalivoda visit www.booksbyhelena.ca.

*I am dedicating this series to my family
and to all who are searching to reconnect
with that part of Divinity we call Self.*

CONTENTS

ACKNOWLEDGEMENT

I thank my incarnate and spiritual muses for their presence in my life. I deeply appreciate the help I have received from Agnes L. Kirby, and I thank her for her unwavering support in the editing of my series of *Purposeful Mind* books.

My appreciation goes to my husband, for his paintings of trees that I used for the book covers of this series and for his understanding of my requirement for my private time when I write.

Helena Kalivoda

PREFACE

Metamorphosis, the last of five books in the empowering and enlightening *Purposeful Mind* series, is intended to help you further expand your awareness essential to your spiritual development. This diverse collection of universal theories and principles retains its transformative influences of the previous books of this series.

I have been receiving guidance from the Spirit world for over fifteen years. In my books, I share what Spirit has shared with me. My hope is that through reading the *Purposeful Mind* series, you will deepen your understanding of being a Spirit embodied on Earth, transcending your duality-based consciousness.

Helena Kalivoda

THE FORM DOES NOT RULE WHO YOU ARE

The form is not the norm.
The form does not rule who you are,
as you are what you always will be,
you are a King that has a Soul.

Do understand that you are a being
that reaches beyond stars,
that is flowing fluidly from one level to another.
That does not know any boundaries,
that is limitless and is full of joy.

Remember, you are not ever different.
All you can accomplish somewhere else
you can accomplish here as well,
as you always are a Soul
that is a loving, thinking being
that is taking on different forms.

Those forms are an outside expression.
Those forms do not change the core.
Those forms are the way of living
and expressing the joy of knowing
that you are a Goddess changing her garb
to suit the occasion,
to suit the story of her undertaking,
to suit the way she wants to evolve.

SELF-RESPECT

Malady is self-brought from self-respect
or rather a lack of it.
If self-respect is not present
then it is shown as malady.
If self-respect is not depreciating
then you are doing well.
When self-respect is optimal,
your health is optimal.

How do you recognize
that you are doing yourself harm?
You can tell from the blotches on your past.
You can tell from your visage.

If it is tired and looks haggard,
you are not respecting yourself.
If it is lively and pleasing
then you are very well appeasing yourself,
and you are doing well in all other aspects,
such as your health and other quality checks.

RENAISSANCE

Renaissance. What is it?
Is it a new age? Is it a rebirth of Christ?
It is a vital mass
of people who are proud to say,
yes, we belong this way.
We belong to this clan,
this clan of all who are not at all afraid
to do their own things at their own pace,
who are not at all fearful of consequences.

La-la-la, la-la-la, let's sing a joyful song.
Let's sing an evolutionary tune,
la-la-la, la-la-la.
All, of the coming golden era, are singing.
All of faith and hope are listening.
They are a beautiful treasure chest
full of shiny spiritual things.

Elevate yourself
with the subdued elegance of thought
that is spiritual, that is of highest mass,
thought that does not dwindle
into inactivity,
but is of creative powers
that result in beauty.

Reach for the stars and to the mass
of Consciousness that is heavenly.
Reach toward your own creator and maker,
your Goddess and God.

GOD IS WITHIN, GOD IS WITHOUT

God that is in you, within, and also without,
that God is here to support you.
That God is clear on your needs,
that God is an omnipotent being,
a primordial mass that is spewing and heaving,
that is kneeling and getting up at the same time.

God is within and God is without.
God is here on Earth wherever you are.
Wherever you go, He is with you.
He is within you as He is you,
and He is also without.

COMMITMENT IS RESPECT FOR YOURSELF

Commitment is not measured by submission.
Commitment is not measured by adulation.
Commitment is not measured by listening to
others.

Commitment is respect for yourself,
respect for your plans and ideas,
respect for your point of view,
respect for your unending stream
that is pulling you up,
up, in an unending mystery
to your starry origin.
Your starry origin that is calling you,
your starry origin that is beckoning you.

Your way throughout the Universe
is not concluded yet.
Commitment is respect
and responsibility to yourself.

KINDNESS AND FORGIVENESS

Kindness and forgiveness
create high vibrations.
They are of love's nature.
They are powerful in creating a new venture
into relationships with people.

Aggressiveness, on the other side,
has a diminishing effect upon your mind.
It is discordant with godly, loving tools.
It does not give you a boost.
It does not make you popular.
It creates a vacuum around you,
it is of a diminishing value.

Determine the value you want to project.
Do it constantly.
And then suddenly, you will realize
that you can go on forever without barriers,
as you are using the true ways
of interacting with people.

Be aware of this truth.
Be aware of the consequences.
Kindness and forgiveness
create high vibrations.
They are of love's nature.

REQUEST COOPERATION

Blessings are not given, they are taken.
Blessings are worked out and received.
Blessings are yours to have
if you initiate them,
when you recognize that you are given
the will to choose and ask.

Request co-operation of the gods.
If you need help, request their help.
Request their help
if you don't know how to proceed.
Ask the gods to intervene on your behalf.
You don't have to feel lonely and lost.

What is it you need to say?
Just ask for help. That is all.
Just say, my dear God,
come to my assistance.
Help me in this endeavour.
Thank you for helping me in this task,
for bringing peace to my mind,
for being with me at all times.

ENTERTAIN MY WISH

Know that the apocalypse is coming
only if you wish,
as your life is what you make it.
Life is a story you weave.
Life is who you are.

So, why don't you just wish and say:
I am here, and please may you
my God, my companion,
entertain my wish,
and please can you make it swift
as the waiting is not
what I need to do any more.

LESS EFFORT AND MORE CREATIVITY

The world can be
an intersection of moving parallel views.
You can see as a physical person
or as a creative spirit muse.

If you say, I am creative
it means your left brain is not working
as much as your right brain,
and to create the balance
you could envision a mathematical problem.

However,
it is not necessary to be always in balance.
If you are domineering on one side
that is perfectly all right.

Monkey says, I am what I see,
then monkey proceeds to do what he sees.
What it sees it repeats,
and that is what makes monkey be.

Less monkey doing, less monkey seeing,
less effort and more creativity
is desired in your life—
effortlessly is a credo to adopt.

An effortless way of living is the way to go.
Less effort and more creativity is desired,
as you are a spiritual being,
and that is the basis of your living.

ALLOW YOURSELF TO BE

Mais oui, mais oui,
all is not as it seems,
all is as it seems.
Which one is true?

Is it your dreams
or your earthly life?
All is true. All is fine.
Stop chasing your tail.
Stop that running around.

Allow yourself to be kind.
Allow yourself to be eclectic.
Allow yourself to be independently wealthy.
Allow yourself to be free.
Allow yourself to be, to be.

CHANGE MUST BE INTERNAL

Change is a way to live.
Stagnancy is not.
Change must be internal,
otherwise, it is a plot.

A plot by you, by others,
to impose the thoughts on those
who are perceived in need of a change.

THE MENTOR

Amnesty is coming through your own doing.
Amnesty is a way of saying
I exclude myself from all
that is not a part of my curriculum.

You are getting close.
You are getting well-coordinated
by a mentor who is from above,
from the above-reaching sky,
who is a heavenly mentor
to help you over your hurdles,
who is a mentor that will calculate the best,
the best time to achieve your goals,
to feel blessed.

Who is that mentor?
Hmm, we thought you knew.
Yes, oh yes, it is you.
You, YourSelf.

THERE IS ONLY ONE WAY

You thirst after Yourself.
You thirst after the knowledge that is yours,
after the knowledge
that is known if you know,
and remote if you don't.

All will come to a halt,
and you will feel like there is a veil.
The Light will come,
and the veil will be lifted
but will not go away.

It will not go away
until you understand
that there is only one way—
your way.

What is 'your way'?
Your way is the way of God,
Your way is the way which is called God
that is in you, that is in all.

You want to lift that veil.
That veil is yours to lift,
as that veil is covering your rise
from Earth to Heaven.

LOVE MATTERS, NOT THE ESOTERIC

Esoteric upbringing is a thing
that allows you to grow faster.
But, esoterically speaking,
esoteric upbringing is not that important.
Important is the way your life goes,
the way your life unfolds,
the way your life is lived by you,
the way your life is energized by you.

The way you live your life,
esotericism or not,
is a given prerequisite of your becoming.
Esoterically speaking,
if esoteric upbringing takes
your life still can be a fake,
just like it can be a fake with all those
who did not receive their esoteric training.

Life is good when you understand
that love matters, not esotericism.
And that is the whole truth, love matters,
esoterically speaking or not.

THE SOUL IS NURTURED FROM GAIETY

Solemn face is a misgiving.
Happy face is forgiving.
Soul is fed from gaiety.
Soul is fed, and in its entirety,
Soul is the last stop for you
to lay your head and rest.

Soul is your friend.
Soul is your fabulous friend
that never left and never will,
that is with you through every ordeal
and through your amazing successes.

SMILE

All you need to do is simple.
Be always ready to put a dimple
on your face. Smile.
That will help you to get a mile,
a mile ahead.

Smile gently.
Yes, like that, it suits you.
Do it quite often.
It will undulate good omens.
It will undulate good feelings.

GIVE YOURSELF THE BEST CHANCE

Brooding face is a sign of beliefs
that are corrupted into fears,
a sign of integrity that is not fully developed
and is about to fold
into a little scared body
that is doing all sorts of moves
to shake the moods.

The moods that will not be shaken
until the fear is forsaken,
and then the beliefs are not blurred
but are clear.

Do not fear. Give yourself the best chance.
It is about your life, about your dreams,
about your passions and wants,
about you, you, you.

Do not brood and do not fear.

VIBRATION

Lethargy is a trait
of people who are afraid.

Positivity is a trait
of people who trust.

Derivation happens
when the thought process is used.

Intuition happens when you listen
to your spiritual muse.

Resonance happens when you vibrate.

Raise your vibration to receive
a direct, clear guidance
from your Higher Self,
from the Universe.

SOLVE THE PUZZLE

Let's solve the puzzle forever.
You and I are Gods.

You are not perceived as Gods,
unless you say you are Gods.

So, then, say it:
you and I are Gods.

Just say it,
and as you do,
you will create it—
that feeling of love
and inner power.

MEDITATING INSTEAD OF WORKING?

How about holding your spot in the Universe
through meditating and contemplating,
instead of always working?

Working is of value if you must.
But comprehend
that you are a child of the Universe
that is called back.

KNOWLEDGE

Knowledge becomes wisdom
when you acquire an understanding
from its application
to how you live.

What you know
can also be a tool that is misused
and then many may be affected and abused.
Knowledge used that way
will eventually backfire.

Knowledge perpetually resurfaces
and at the point of knowing
you may realize, oh yes,
I always have known all this,
as I tap the cumulative knowledge
of the Universes.

TAKE THE REINS INTO YOUR HANDS

As we speak, the night is falling down.
How long will you be as meek as you are?
How long will it take you to understand
that you do not need to defend what you are?

You are a star that shines ever so bright.
You are a star, you are,
and it is your responsibility
to take the reins into your hands
and start a new chapter
where you are not a servant
to any material matter.

THERE IS A NIRVANA WAITING

Be ready to leave the door
that does not lead anywhere,
the door that keeps you here to stay,
the door that you believe is forbidden to open.

It keeps you in a bubble of reality that is not real,
that is imaginary and so surreal
that we keep on wondering
how on earth (and is this a pun or what?)
you can be so fooled that,
that you all are mislead into believing
that your world is a reality
where all is happening.

There is more to see, there is more.
There is a nirvana waiting
that will make the North Pole
out of any vibrant and beautiful place
on Earth.

What is it going to be?
You and your Thee
are waiting for your answer.

COCOON YOU HAVE BEEN

Your commitment to yourself
is a way of finding who you are.
Are you holding yourself hostage
by pretending to you about you,
withholding the information from you
about your true self?

Are you a person who is not very grounded?
Are you a person, who is spiritual?
Are you a person who is not well versed
in spirituality itself?
Are you a person who can climb mountains?
All of those need to be found.

Do not hesitate to ask questions.
Do not hesitate to negotiate
with your Higher Self.
Find who you are.

You can emerge as a cocoon or as a butterfly.
A cocoon you have been for a long time,
it is important to see that butterfly
open its wings and fly.

SPREAD YOUR WINGS

Love yourself. Spread your wings.
Be your own guide, and do not think
that others can change the outcome of your life.
You are a maker, a creator,
of your own universe, of your own realizations,
of all your own palaces and caves.

You can build bridges,
you can topple mountains,
you can change absolutely anything.

You can bring the changes, and you are.
You can accelerate from where you are.
You have absolute power
to do anything you wish—
it is your absolute, absolute power.

I HAVE ALL I NEED

I do not need to suffer doubts any more.
I do not need to agonize and fear.
I am becoming clear on my role.

I am abundant.
I don't need to toil.
I am not in a creed
of toiling any more.

I have all I need.
I have, I believe.
I trust
that the Universe
fulfills all my wants.

ONE IS AS IMPORTANT AS ALL

The Universe is vast
and it has never cast,
cast anyone away.

In casting one away,
the Universe would harm itself,
as one is as important as all.

One is all and all is one.
Do you understand this truth?

THE UNIVERSE

The Universe is a pliable thought pattern.
The Universe is a way
to conduct your business on Earth.

Through the Universe,
you can recall dreams.
You can recall pasts.

You can recall all your needs,
as they appeared,
were fulfilled and disappeared.

YOU DECIDE

How about me?

What about you?

Me, where am I today?
How, when, how fast will I evolve?

We hope soon.
You will decide, not us.

ECHINACEA IT AIN'T

Echinacea's way is a way of prompting
your cells into an action,
is a way of telling your body:
hey, you, body, behave,
give me a good interaction.

There is a trend toward herbs.
There is a trend toward healthy living.
The trend is not, listen, it is not wrong.
However, it all starts with your mind,
from there it is all happening.

Your mind is the creator
of you, your body,
of your actions, your satisfaction,
your failures, your successes.
That, my dear, is very, very clear.
That is the clear message
we would like to convey—
echinacea it ain't.

Echinacea, as a pacifier,
is a way to help your body
and that is all. Down deep in you,
your thoughts are doing all.
Your thoughts, your musings set the stage
and are not, repeat,
are not at this very age,
fully understood.

Echinacea it ain't!

ELEMENTAL KINGDOM

Leprechauns exist, so do faeries,
without any doubt,
as they are a part of another sphere of life.

Gargantuan creatures are alive as well,
and that is not all,
giant creatures are everywhere,
just as are the small.

Why are we writing about that?
Hmm, do you care?
Maybe not, but now and then
it is interesting
to hear stories like that.

NOT ALL CAN BE HEARD AND SEEN

Caramba, boom, saint is flying,
child is crying, not enough milk,
Aristotle is here, peace is near.

Mais oui, mais oui, what was it all about?
Aren't you glad that not all
can be heard and seen?
Imagine if we wouldn't pre-screen,
what all you would be able to hear.

Dandy, as it may seem,
we can lift and pull down the screen
that releases or blocks the noises
of the surrounding Universes.

NATION

A nation is a grouping of people
who came together
to experience similar, the same.
They are together by their choice,
not by their birth—
their birth is predetermined
by their choice.

As a part of nation, they can work out
their aberrations to the extent
that one is learning from the other,
that one is affecting another,
that one is affecting the rest of the matter.
Mass consciousness is created
that is lifting all.

SCIENCE

Science is of a funny nature.
Scientists—they lecture,
they err, they preach,
about the world and its qualities.

The Earth is round,
and yes, we know that,
and electrons are everywhere.
You can be a scientist
but you will not understand
everything about the world.

Science is a sure way of saying,
if we don't see it, then it is not.
If we don't find it, then it is not.
It is not, until we prove it.
It is not, until we discover it.

Science says, well, have it your way,
we are not subscribing to it,
as we did not find it
in our lab.

And meanwhile, all goes on without them.
Then they feel they don't want to miss the train,
and they say, oh, yes, yes, sure,
we knew it all the while.

We knew about electrons
being able traverse an incredible space,
space that isn't measured by earthly measures,

space that is not traveled through,
as it is not three-dimensional.

As the proverbial saying says,
I don't see it, therefore it ain't.

DARWIN

Darwin's theory says an eye for an eye,
a tooth for a tooth, who is strong will win.
But Darwin was not right.
A tooth for a tooth, an eye for an eye,
does not pay.
Small consolation, you say.

Darwin missed the fact that all is intact
and evolving as one mass.
All are linked, all are connected,
all are appreciatively aware of each other,
all are one big, big Consciousness
that has many forms,
that has many ways of expressions,
that has its own deity that is itself,
and knows that itself is God.

Darwin missed that
in his elaborate theory,
as he did not account for the way
the mass is thinking of itself,
and that the mass' elements
are aware of each other.
They know that you are their brother,
because you are that mass.

That mass is a primordial soup
that became complex,
that is evolving and has always had a context.
Its context was God that is within
you and me. He is within all.

INDUSTRIAL CAVE

Once you were a cave dweller
who today lives in an industrial cave.

An industrial cave is a hindrance.
You must not forget that it is a cave,
where all doings need to be within a norm
and are not to be challenged too much,
are not to be challenged.

You are challenging, you are questioning.
You are subsequently getting or not getting
your answer.

You are not convinced
that all that is said has to be adhered to,
that others are right and you are not,
that all are seeing and you cannot.

You are questioning your need to live in a cave.
You are questioning your listening to those
who are not letting themselves live in a way
that does not include their industrial caves.

Free yourself from any caves.
No industrial caves. No caves of any kind.
No caves that say this is the way to live,
and you obey what you hear,
and you do not interpret your feelings,
and you do not use your free will,
but you aimlessly listen to those
who are closed in their caves.

MESMERIZED IS THE WORLD

Mesmerized is the world by technology,
mesmerized is the world.

Mesmerism is a thing
that can take you to the brink,
to the brink of a disaster,
such as millennia ago,
when the world was round
and disaster came
and then the world became
somewhat elliptical.

Neglect of the spiritual side
allows human kind
to experience vibrations
that are not all that pleasant.
Such, as a long time ago,
Atlantis lost so much ground
that it sank
and disappeared from sight.

Atlantis was a measure of satisfaction,
technologically speaking.
However, the spiritual aspect was lost.
The spiritual aspect gives you meaning,
as you are a spiritual being.

You, as a spiritual being,
cannot deny yourself the fact
that spirituality is the way
to lead your life.

In denial of your birthright,
you bring disasters to your homeland,
to the Earth.

The Earth, as your homeland, is very precious.
It is a beautiful place.
It is a place of joys and sorrows.
It is a place of whispers and shouts.
It is a place of dark and heavy,
soft and light.

Take care,
take care of your Mother Earth.

RELIGION

Once you become a member of a sect,
'religion' is mandatory,
and it smacks of treachery
every time you say something different
or contrary.

But you, your own leader,
do not need religious talk,
as you do not need to become a part
of an organized religion.
You do not need to think like others.
You do not need to sing what they sing.

You are an individual,
and at the same time
you are also a part
of one Soul,
of one being.

SHIP

Ship is rocking on its own waves
created by its own movement,
just as you are rocking
to the tune of your thoughts.

SIMPLE

Profound truth is simple.
It is simple and understandable.
That is why it is truth.

A TREE OF LIFE

A tree of life is a multidimensional maze.
It is not linear.

BANALITY

Banality pursued stays banal.
What is it you are pursuing?

GESTALT

Gestalt is when all comes together
and creates more than what is
when added together.
Gestalt is a beautiful way of saying,
you have arrived.

You have arrived. You are home.
You are connected and you know.
You can be here and there,
you can know the future and the past.
You can have a blast
anywhere from where you are.

EMERALD

Emerald is the colour of your face
when it lights up with the joy of knowing
that you are liking what you are doing.

Emerald is a heart that you carry.
Emerald is a pair of binoculars
that allow you to see the fog firstly,
then clear days ahead.

Emerald is a colour that you flow into,
as emerald signifies your hopes,
your thoughts, your overall disposition.

Green is a colour of healing.
Emerald, emerald, emerald[1].

---

[1] The author's friend shared that as she read the above poem
she remembered that one night some years ago when she
looked at the author, the author was glowing a bright green
colour. The author believes what her friend saw was the
colour of her aura system.

YOUR HEART IS GREEN

Blue, as it seems to be, blue is the sky.
Green, as it seems to be, is your heart.
Your heart is green as it should be,
as being green is an expression of faith and value,
as green is your colour,
your colour is green.

Do allow yourself to become even greener.
Improve your love and compassion,
as it is in your fashion
sometimes to be stubborn and unyielding.
Do become even greener,
do go within to discover who you are.

Go within.

It sounds nice and easy,
but how do you do it without feeling queasy?

Well, there are methods
and then there are surprises.
We don't know which you choose,
and you know that you lose
if you are expecting someone to tell you,
as your experiences are yours to have.

YOUR NOTIONS ABOUT YOURSELF

Relationships are a way of testing
your notions about yourself.

If you are successful in relationships,
you are successful at being at ease
with yourself.

FAME

Claim to fame, what does that mean?
Fame is not an element to be stuck on.
Fame is misunderstood by those
who claim that famous is the way to be.

Famous is a way not to be.
Quiet understanding and knowledge is the way.
Fame is to be stuck in the foreground,
to be ogled and on view,
and that is not where you want to be.

Your way is just to be.
Claim to fame is not important to you.
Important is that you contribute to others and you.
To you, fame is of no importance.

LAZY

At all times when you say, I am lazy,
you mean that you cannot comprehend
why you need to work at this and that.

Do not think that you need
to apologetically say, well, I am so lazy.
What you mean is, yes,
I acknowledge that it is needed
but I don't think it is important.

Just make it into your kind of a day.
Enjoy the day the way you wish to,
enjoy the way you know to make it yours.
You do not need to say, here, look at me,
I am having a good day, as I am a bit lazy.

There is no shame to being lazy
if that's what you need.
The creed is not to say it apologetically
as that makes it into a 'sin' situation
and that will be in a violation
of your basic rights to be
who and what you are.

LEADERSHIP

Leadership is a big, underestimated act,
that is not fully understood.

Leadership is when you, as a leader, say,
have a very good day.
I have this and this to do today,
you Pam, you Jackie, please lead the way.

It is not what you may think it is.
It is not a despotic
or desperate claim of your powers.
It is a balance of wisdom and leadership
that is carrying you and your team
toward your goals.

PARABLE

You are climbing to Heaven and you fall.
You get hurt and you say it is God's fault.

God is omnipotent, but you are your own guide.
God is kind, but you are your own judge.

POVERTY IS NOT

Poverty is not
what you would like to experience in your life.
Poverty is a destiny you are not planning for.
Poverty is not an interesting way of life,
and you are not about to become poor.

Poor in relationships, poor in love,
poor in friendships,
poor about how you live and breathe,
how you think and sleep.
That is not the way you love or think.

UNCONDITIONAL LOVE

How do you love or love not
those who are tall or not that tall?
How do you love or love not
those who are small or not that small?
How do you love or love not
those who are fat or not that fat?

Do you love all equally, unconditionally?
Not all can be perceived the same.
Not all can be looking the same.
Not all can be asking the same questions.
Not all can be playing the same game.
Yet, all is one.

ELIMINATE WASTE

Eliminate the waste
that is cluttering your space.
Diligently work through the piles of waste.
Diligently work toward it now,
for organization, for a specific order of things,
for malnutrition of wrong habits,
for clarity of mind.

Encountering clarity of mind
depends on cleanliness of a kind
that you usually do not connect
with your unlearned understanding
that the clutter of physical things
is cluttering your mind.

The cluttered mind is not able
to be clear and kind,
and then it clutters more
your physical space,
your environment.

Be good to yourself
through creating a space
that is bemusedly clean and healthy,
and is not a place
that is full of clutter and messy.

YOU ARE A WOMAN

You are a woman.
You are a live, live woman.
A woman that is wise and discerning,
who reaches out for the Universe.

You are a woman that is on her path.
You are a woman who is not
sulking, crying, hurting,
who is well aware of her dreams,
who is well aware of the songs she sings,
who is well aware.

ADAM AND EVE

When Adam and Eve were born
they were given powers
to understand their own godly nature.

They forgot
that their body is a body
which could traverse dimensions.

They forgot
that love was about
upholding a spiritual body.

Please understand
that you are the ones
who created and bent
your own life story,
and the dense earthly body
has forgotten the feeling
of expansive joy
and freedom everlasting.

ASCENSION

Ascension is a Christ happening
that is of important significance,
as humanity en masse
will be fully encompassed
by their I AM Presence.

You will raise your consciousness
and are different from those in the past
as you will ascend en masse,
not as the earlier masters,
who ascended one by one.

ASCETIC WAY OF LIFE

An ascetic way of life is the way of immortality,
is a way of preserving your Soul.
An ascetic way of life
does not mean neediness or poverty.

It is in an understanding of your needs.
It is in an understanding of your wants.
It is in an understanding
of your anecdotal earthly lives
that come and go,
that are surviving your tremendous urges
to join us forever and ever.

KNOW HOW TO

Be aware of two things—
yourself and others.
What others do
is not as important as what you do.

Life is simple and beautiful
when you know how to.
How to train yourself not to be
so sensitive to outside influences.

How to be ready to act.
How to do what you can
to uplift yourself and then
how to be when your worlds
start coming apart.

DON'T BE A LITTLE WORM

Don't be like a little bug
that is as useful as it is smug,
as it thinks it is on the brink
of a new discovery.
So it crawls, so it digs,
so it pushes and it heaves,
until it is back to where it started from.

Raise your vibrations.
Raise your salutations
to your God within.
Don't be like a little worm
that is pushing and heaving.
Be sure that you will not come
to where you started from.

AS YOU ARE INWARDLY

The indication may be
that it is an influence from outside.
However,
it is your belief interpreting outside.

As you are inwardly
that is how outside is reflected by you.
As you are inwardly,
that is how you relate to others
and that is how they relate to you.

NEVER MIND

Mais oui, mais oui, here we are again.
We are attaching to your thought train.
We are your friends and relatives,
we are your guides.
We came to say,
please never mind.

Never mind
if life seems not what you want.
All has its own time.
All is not what it is on the surface.
All is as you designed it yourself
through your thoughts.

Listen to your ways of thinking.
Listen to your intuition.
Be your own guide and a preacher,
and then you don't have to pay any tuition,
as you are your own teacher.

NEVER RESIST ANY OPPORTUNITY

Benevolent entity,
place this on your to do list.

Place there: never resist.
Never resist any opportunity,
opportunity to cry or smile,
opportunity to sell or buy,
opportunity to rest your head down.

SELECTIVE THINKING

Selective breeding is not the answer,
selective thinking is.

What you think, you are.
What you perceive is the result.

HOW IS IT GOING?

How is it going for you?
Do you feel trapped?
Do you feel unappreciated?
Do you feel bewildered?
Do you feel perplexed?
Is it all in your head?

Naturally.
As you think, you are.

LIVE IN THE PRESENT

Live a day-to-day life
without a thought about
what was
and what will happen tomorrow.

TRAVESTY

Travesty is when you say
I cannot do it, but you don't try.
Travesty is when you say
I am not interested, but you still pry.

Travesty is when there is a surge of energy
that is coming from below and above
and you are not appreciative
and are asking for more and more.

Travesty is when all is given to you
and you are not acting as advised.

HITLER

Was Hitler an individual from hell?
No, he was not, as he was formed
by the whole mass consciousness.
He was a result of the thoughts
that were heaving in his
and other people's minds.

Was he a victim?
No, not at all.
He had a free choice
to become that or the other.
He became what he chose,
and that was his impact, his contribution
to the whole consciousness evolution.

He took the choice that was already in existence
and then he had persistence
in carrying it on.

BEWARE OF THE IDENTITY OF THE CALLER

Once upon a time, there was a lovely girl.[2]
She became engaged to the earthly plane.
She was married to many earthly problems,
then visited us and discovered the truth.

She is struggling and is trying to move,
her feet are stuck in a goo
of earthly molasses.

Unlisted has been her number
and it is becoming listed
in the phone book of the Universe.
She needs to be careful whom she answers,
as this is an important time in her life.
She needs to be beware of the identity of the caller.

These verses are about you
and you need to say:
Who are you?
Are you good or evil?
And then do as you feel you need to do.
If in doubt do not answer,
as this is a crucial point
of your development.

---

[2] At the time when the author was new at receiving messages
from Spirit, the above poem came as a warning for her to use
discernment when receiving such communications. This may
apply to others who are opening themselves to interacting
with entities existing beyond this physical dimension.

ANGELS

Angels are standing by you.
Angels are heralding your triumphs.
Angels are doing what you are doing.
They are looking for the truth,
looking for the objects that do not belong,
looking for a way to amass
the gold of love and happiness.

YOU ARE FROM THE STARS

You are from the stars.
You are from Mars.
You are from Pleiades.
You are from far and wide.

You are star children, you are.
And this is how you know
where you came from:
by this feeling of awe about the stars
that are hanging above you
and are colliding at times
and are so beautiful,
and are, are, are.

YOU ARE MADE OF STARDUST

You are made of stardust
that was cast into a human form.
The stardust is like fog,
the stardust is so filmy.
All flesh, all bones,
are of stardust,
eons, eons ago.

Gusts of the cosmic wind
blew the stardust together.
Gusts of the cosmic wind,
at God's will,
did bring the dust together
and humanity was born.

The feat took millennia to form.
This feat and other feats
that are happening
and will happen in the future,
are God's will,
the Creator's will.

BECOME A STAR OF DAVID

Human, as an animal,
is rising
toward a big uprising
when all will collapse
and a true jewel
will come out
in a very lively way.

When human will end his animal ways,
he will become a Star of David.
He will become another Soul
that knew itself,
that came aboard,
that found its way home.

Home sweet home,
home of many stars,
home of all the stardust,
that became Souls
created in the image of Creator, of God,
God that is loving and kind.

God, who is omnipotent.
God, who is all that you need to know.
God who is, was, and will be.

HUMANS ARE A SPECIFIC BRAND

Humans are not too commonly seen
in other parts of the Universe.

Humans are a specific brand of starry beings
that were congealed into matter,
and reflect their inane believing
that matter is all they can have
and can be seeing.

SPIRITUALITY IS A GIVEN

Pleasures of life are what we see
when we are born to this Earth.
Pleasures of life are on our minds.

Pleasures of flesh are the ones we crave.
Pleasures of the mind are those
we may have or not,
as that is based on what we know
or do not.

Sensual part of us is ready to experience.
Mindful part is ready to analyze.
And what about our spiritual side,
where does that reside?

Our spiritual part is hidden from sight.
It is hidden as you rise to seek it.
You can be smart but that it is not what it takes
to find your spiritual side.

Spirituality is a given
and that is all we can say.
And then you may or may not believe
that you are made of spiritual ray.

YOU CANNOT NEED

Your mind is steeped in this plane
and your third eye is a gateway
that shines through to other worlds.

To pass through this gateway
you'd better, and remember this,
you'd better abandon your needs.

You cannot need to be beautiful or ugly.
You cannot envy.
You cannot think thoughts that may harm others.
You cannot abdicate from your earthly charges.

You, however, may become the one
who believes that Earth is the place
to understand spirituality
by speaking gently,
by speaking wisely,
by not being crass,
by learning to give your time.

Now is the time to come and say,
I am a spiritual being, I am.
I am a spiritual being that is here on this Earth
to comprehend and to help comprehend
why life is the way it is.

TRUTH

Blizzard, dark.
All of a sudden, sun.
Sun that is warm, life giving.
That is how it feels
when you know the truth.

What is the truth?
Is it something you know?
Is it something
that is unchanging and static?

The truth is a living thing.
Yet, it is unchanging in its entirety,
as all basic truths are always valid,
such as being truthful and joyful,
such as honesty.

SUFFERING IS OUT

Stoic heroism of suffering is out.
Joy is in.
Stoic, slow dying of unhappiness is out.
Love and exuberance are in.

Enjoy yourself and please yourself
whenever you feel.
This is how you want to live
your day.

JOY

Joy is receiving pleasure from your actions.
Joy is an interaction with your spiritual mind.
Joy is a way of saying,
oh, God, I am so glad
I met you again
today.

ABOUT THE AUTHOR

Helena Kalivoda is an award-winning author devoted to sharing inspirational messages that support readers in transforming their lives. Lives of peace and happiness can be available to those who learn the power of creation through an open heart as encouraged by Helena's books.

AWAKEN! Spirit Is Calling, Helena's first book, contains powerful truths for each person's journey. These poignant teachings were downloaded from Helena's spirit guides.

Her second book, *WAKE UP! Your Heart Is Calling,* leads readers to realize that all aspects of humanity, when denied pure love, are bound to eventually fail and cannot be healthy. This book connects to an online environment where you can access extended resources to help you apply the learned principles.

WAKE UP! Prosperity Is Calling, Helena's third book, outlines The Seven Principles to Living a Life of Prosperity. These principles will become your truth and experience once you use them and live them consistently.

Recently, Helena completed her new series of *Purposeful Mind* books of poetry. *Metamorphosis* is the last book of this series.

Helena holds a BA in Economics and B.Sc. in Computer Science. She is a mother of three, living in Canada. In 1997, she left the corporate world to continue the writing she started in the early nineties.

Visit www.booksbyhelena.ca for more information about Helena Kalivoda's books.